The Llŷn Writings

Also by Peter Riley:

Poetry
Love-Strife Machine
The Canterbury Experimental Weekend
The Linear Journal
The Musicians, The Instruments
Preparations
Lines on the Liver
Tracks and Mineshafts
Ospita
Noon Province
Sea Watches
Reader
Lecture
Sea Watch Elegies
Royal Signals
Distant Points
Alstonefield
Between Harbours
Noon Province et autres poèmes
Snow has settled ... bury me here
Author
Passing Measures: A Collection of Poems
The Sea's Continual Code
Aria with Small Lights
Alstonefield (extended edition)
Excavations
A Map of Faring
The Day's Final Balance: Uncollected Writings 1965-2006

Prose
Two Essays
Company Week
The Dance at Mociu

The Llŷn Writings

Peter Riley

Shearsman Books
Exeter

First published in the United Kingdom in 2007 by
Shearsman Books Ltd
58 Velwell Road
Exeter EX4 4LD

www.shearsman.com

ISBN-13 978-1-905700-15-8

ISBN-10 1-905700-15-6

Copyright © Peter Riley, 1991, 1993, 1996, 2000, 2003, 2007.

The right of Peter Riley to be identified as the author of this work has been asserted by him in accordance with the Copyrights, Designs and Patents Act of 1988. All rights reserved. No part of this publication may be reproduced, stored in a retrieval system, transmitted in any form or by any means, electronic, mechanical, photocopying, recording or otherwise, without the prior permission of the publisher.

Acknowledgements
Parts of this book first appeared as follows:
Sea Watches. Prest Roots Press 1991; *Sea Watch Elegies*. Poetical Histories, 1993; *Between Harbours*. An artist's book by Colin Whitworth, Cambridge 1996; *Passing Measures: a collection of poems*. Carcanet 2000; *The Sea's Continual Code*. An artist's book by Colin Whitworth, Cambridge 2003; and in issues of *The Gig, PN Review, Skald,* and *Europe*.

Thanks are due to Peter Larkin, Colin Whitworth, Michael Schmidt, Nate Dorward, Ian Davidson and Lorand Gaspar, and to all those involved in these histories, and special thanks to Michael Haslam who first told us about Llŷn.

The author and publisher are grateful to Carcanet Press Limited for permission to reprint 'Sea Watches', 'Sea Watch Elegies' and 'Between Harbours' from *Passing Measures* by Peter Riley (2000).

The publisher gratefully acknowledges financial assistance from
Arts Council England.

Contents

1. Sea Watches — 7

2. Six Prose pieces (1977-80)
   - St Merin's church (i) — 27
   - St Merin's church (ii) — 28
   - St Merin's churchyard — 29
   - A spring on the upper slopes of Mynedd Anelog — 30
   - In a white van . . . — 31
   - Rhwngyddwyborth, 6th September . . . — 32

3. Poems and notes (1980-5)
   - 'fixed points in succession . . .' — 35
   - Dithyrambic, after the Vicar of Aberdaron — 36
   - 'Ptolemy on Llŷn . . .' — 37
   - 'Late autumn, the peninsula on the turn . . .' — 38
   - Porth Gwrtheyrn — 39
   - A Repetition of Machado at Porth Gwrtheyrn — 40
   - Porth y Nant — 41

4. Sea Watch Overstock (1984-9)
   - Pieces, fragments, and notes . . . — 45
   - The Nightwatch Notebook — 47

5. Mornings with a Walkman at Rhwngyddwyborth (1989-90) — 53
   - Things Saying Themselves in Llŷn (1990) — 56

6. Sea Watch Elegies — 59

7. The Translations of St. Columba's Sea-Watch — 67

8. Overheard by the Sea — 71

9. Between Harbours — 75

10. Six small prose pieces formerly attached to 'Between Harbours' (1994) — 85

11. Absent from Llŷn 1994-1997: four prose poems — 89

12. Llŷn in the Rain, September 1998	97
Only the Song	103
13. Llŷn, Pausing and Going	105
Addenda and Notes to 'Sea Watches'	111
Bibliography	123

1

Sea Watches

I. CLIFF-TOP ANNUALS

1
Almost there we hesitate, and turn, high on the soft
Edge of Britain, to view the whole story: the sea barking
Up both sides of the peninsula to the point, top
Crest of land, pilgrims' goal or final extent
Of a life's coming and going called together when
There is after all a focus, an intellectual love.

2
That we shall not reach today and is quite
Obviously already all we are, and warns us
Not to postpone the issue for a quiet bed
Or any other future. The car gentle as a hearse
Takes sunken roads through fields that carry
Sea-glow, yellow scatter, proud, tall and thin.

3
Grey concrete road down old stream cleft
To the bay, white sand, slab sea, guard dog barking,
Chug of generator engine at the beach shop:
Unchanged items. And the same us with different
Surfaces, year after year we are here again.
Alternatim to eternity, if our love is proven.

4.
Wide and bright sea spread in the great daylight,
Dividing behind to the isolated fires that warm us.
Stone shore where the light breaks. A marble boulder, red
Veins in the white mist, smooth watery surface
Half sunk in grey sand, so hard and clear a thing that
We are put to guess what harm we could be in.

5
Shifting slow and vast extent viewed from the cliff
Top, so large as to raise questions talking
Of the whole of a life not just now and never to stop
Forgetting the recent deceits of resentment.
So calm and clear a thing as not to be around when
The earth is lost to those of mere power.

6
Closed earthlumps that collide together and fight
In the dark we seem, and the seeming harms us.
Yet we retain moments of casual success as we feed
The family in the caravan at a meal-time close to others',
Hid from the noisily munching ocean that
Thrusts behind my ear like a jewelled hat-pin.

7
Pyramids of light flickering on and off
On the sea surface, wedges of light, and us walking
Back to sleep on the abandoned table-top
Like the horizon's dinner. But instrumental
Day and night for intercourse of love and pain.
The hills bend their heads to the hollow, homely hour.

8
Half crying sea birds above us in the night,
The constant breath of wind and the farmer's
Wife comes out with a little torch to feed
The geese. Baffled at yet another mother's
Triumph the sky stamps its foot and raises its hat
And charges out to sea rattling its tin.

II. Sandlogged

1
A double track, a furrow in the groundswell
From the house down to the sea, a corrugated breach
Between fields of sheep and wheat, down to the great sink.
Lined with hawthorn, bramble, blackthorn, bent
Gorse: Look how the wasps wallow in their graves,
Bathing in ripe blackberries, drinking their blood!

2
On either hand the seething fields and the full sea
Like life and death (though which is which)
And stark on the margin between them crowds
Of people, blurring over the sands like brush-
strokes, shouting and lying. You'd never believe
The cadences, the successions of fall.

3
Fields of wheat and pasturage halting at the level
Sea, where the fish shoals move in and out of reach.
And the beach crowd fills the bay with truce flags, pink
Blue and yellow, choral energy, manes iridescent
In the sunlight. And voices over the crashing waves,
Calling us out to face our enemies, gods of food.

4
Beyond the pleasure zone the cormorants skim steadily
Over their door to success crying at a pitch
Of failure (this is the solitary walk between crowds
On the clifftop pastures) and those crazy birds rush
To and from their island capital, unable to deceive
Themselves out of constant pleasure, constant thrall.

5
Souls of the crowd chorusing like a bell
Of a clifftop church, clear over grass and rocks, each
To each extolling what we have and like to think
Even despair is a shrewdness, a gesture meant
To spread the load. But, *das einsam,* ah, he craves
Gem-like contraries in the wrack, eyes in the dark hood.

6
Cooling and getting hungry we slowly
Walk back along the long sands carrying beach-
balls, blankets, fish-nets, binoculars, crabs,
Two small girls, books, towels, pebbles to keep, brush
And comb, bucket and spade; we carry what we conceive,
We carry carrying, being carried, fear and fatigue, we carry it all.

7
"I was ill, I couldn't sleep, I couldn't tell
What I was doing, so I came to this remote stretch
Of coast to fight the falsest persons I could think…"
And the sea this evening calm, a seething tent
Of blue-grey down smeared salmon and thick with caves.
Duplicitous, occultly tumultuous, screen of blood.

8
Almost asleep in the thin walls, undeliberately
I send my soul out like a night bird or a witch
To fly over the dark roads now silent of cars
And kids, skimming over the fields and black bushes
Over the white line that the wild waves weave
To settle on the headland, with your moon I fall.

III. Sailing, Sailing Away

1
Cold and wet, shout out the morning news:
No unit of life's pain will be eased this day
Or by being out here. The wind and the rain
Comb the field grass and units of time past
Rattle in our heads like pellets. Then space
Partitions and new warm promises crackle in our beaks.

2
Hell's Mouth. We scuttle across it in pairs.
We are traders: offerers, losers, those who
Claim to be givers are the worst of all.
Vast arc of shore where the sea never stops
Pounding the sand, days nights and years away.
Drear infinity. We cluster back to the car and lunch.

3
Next we stride across acres of jagged wet rocks and bruise
Insteps through the rubber. We get across the bay
Limping from shelf to shelf. There are departments of pain,
I suppose, and stores and garages. Our memories are massed
Against us but we slip them by in the trusty face
Of the arched instant. The car engine sputters into ticks.

4
Up and down the small valley the slow soft airs
Come to and fro, the stream purls and slips through
Old manganese workings: here and there a ruined wall,
Black holes in the valley sides. A stone dropped drops
Through nothing to distant water. And remember, far away
From here management decides hurt. Thank you, Mr Punch.

5
Why do we roam the land as if finding and lose
Everyone's time? There is nothing, but a grey
Gravel, a lost horizon, and a winding rain.
The slightest construct of care would cast
It all behind us like salt as we turn to face
A clearing sky to landward and a truly human fix.

6
Out on the open sea in a small boat there's
Suddenly nothing that isn't obviously true.
The sea top is a shining cloth. A dying gull
Sits in it like an old man in an armchair, props
A wing on the meniscus and joins the lift and sway,
Slowly giving himself to the one truth for ever head first.

7
The boat glides up the cove and grates on the loose
Stones. We mount the side cliff and wind up the day
In wet shoes with fishscales in our hair. The fisherman
Winds the boat up the shore, grinding slowly past
Heaps of marine detritus and wrack, to a safe place.
The light is almost gone. The sky curtain stirs and leaks.

8.
Lying dozing late in the dark caravan, slight glares
Of lighthouse in a square on the ceiling, every few
Moments, I send my consciousness out like a gull
Over the sea, away from the wasteful and gaudy shops
Of this life, away from my own tricks, indeed away
From the untruthful land. This dark divided church.

IV. Forth Out and First Back

1
Driving up the coast road alone, a strange sense
Of being already dead, suspended where I pass
Over hills and through villages, incapable of harm
Or good to the people. My wish is neutral of course,
Provisional good sincerely upon unknown heads.
At a bad cliff corner the family leaps in my throat.

2
And on up the side of North Wales to a town
Selling death back to the lost people from industry
As coloured wrap with glims of distance, toffee stick,
And here-we-are-before-we-were-again (pastoral) that slides
Off before you can suck it. So buy quick and go,
On by the cool straits, the calm woods, and railways.

3
A country is no one's playground, no one's absence.
The mountains gather towards the sea, touched with thin grass,
And the coastal strip sweeps under in a curling arm.
A country must be sure to be more than a pause
In a life or a year. Pecking at the scattered threads
Of a remote history, small salt crystals stick to my coat.

4
The car park at Bethesda is roof height on the first crown
Of the valley side. I get out of the car and am instantly
In a large arena of lost industry, black scarp, headline nick:
Broken backed mountains and the sky stock full of clouds slides
Constantly over. Fears and promises flicker across us
Like shadow angels. We cleave between. Oh razor-sharp days!

5
Returning shortly to the car park at Bethesda the tense
Distance of farms and cottage rows on high shelves
Of the slate mountain, hit by the late sun, calm
And empty one senses an enemy. There is a torse
In the pastoral disc, an incision at the quarry beds
Letting through the dark. The day's width offers a groat.

6
There is an exit, a return. The road leads down
Into the valley, up and over this shifting, sliding geography
The car shoots past chapels and fortresses as quick
As a thought about where the enemy bides,
The false person I wanted to have a go
At. Cloven hillsides and the gulls flying sideways.

7
Nothing but evasion. I am in the men's
At Tudweiliog, a tourist pub, thinking alas
I cannot define the root of harm without alarm
But I'm glad we sit together at the tables among gorse
Bushes children's swings and flower beds.
Brave harmony, from heaven's blast remote.

8
I squeeze my eyes and I'll blow your house down
Says the wind banging all night with blustery
Threat the tin panels of the caravan I'll kick
It to bits says the wind and life it rocks from side
To side and my mind is miles away in the still slow
Garden at the roots of the wind the voicing maze.

V. Performing Dogs

1
Triangular field, pointing out to sea
Like an open beak, grass crown, feathery cliffs,
Grazed thin, scattered with white flecks:
Feathers, wool, thistledown; I walk you this morning
End to end wondering how a new day won't reach more
Than an inch or two forwards or raise its head above shame.

2
So hive off on an excuse. Green road, hilltop ruins.
The solitary on the top track, fearful of farm dogs,
Pauses before the uninhabited, holiday cottage.
The wind is everywhere, the house another family's
Mindstock: childhood coin and wedding gift and
Promised past. Curtains closed. God save us from death.

3
Or the great shore empty as far as you can see
Curving away, the waves grinding the quarried cliffs
Roaring into shingle, difficult walking, slow steps
Across the wind. Which if it led or were pointing
Anywhere would be a happy place, if the stones bore
Down the chute and rattled into boats under a trade name.

4
At Nefyn the travelling circus chimes and spins
The same old tale with its ropes and its dogs
As any other twisting mirror: that age in age
Out we detest what we become, and were, we hiss
And bark in the big pointed tent, we can't stand
Our ends and gladly hoot a fearsome breath.

5
God save us from half-life, it is also necessary
To note, sitting on the rocks eating fish and chips
At twilight, on the edge of the great curve, six
Mile bay watching people zooming and spinning
And riding the meniscus to what point or
Purpose we don't know but working all the same.

6
To their renown, for each is a space that wins
Its own centre, to which you and I are just dogs
Perhaps, just a circus game on the far edge
Of visibility. And some spin quietly and miss
Reward, but turn an acre of inhospitable land
Into a terraced garden, richly flawed, flowered, brief.

7
Love is where centres meet, I think I see,
Gathering mushrooms at twilight on the high cliff
Pastures, those white domes glowing like clocks
Here and there on the dark ground and the dawning
Sea light over my shoulder and they don't just grow or
Gravitate. But beam and echo name to name.

8
Lying awake at night my focus climbs
To the caravan skylight, barking dogs
At the farm, slowly, like old age
Mounting into a mortgaged tower, to kiss
The ghost of distance behind a shadow hand
And watch the sea, and stick there, weathered leaf.

VI. Eaten Zero

1
Sometimes pasts are satisfied. It's like
Sitting on a café terrace over the deserted shore
In the evening sunlight sipping coffee in the thin
Savoury smoke of a barbecue as the waves reach
And reach in white fuss the great length
Of brown sands, where no claims reside.

2
The man who runs the beach shop and café at Porth Or
Decided one year to stay open in the evenings
And run a barbecue. No one came but it was
A gentle evening of deep sun and enough wind
From the sea to ruffle one's hair and move
An empty cardboard plate across the table.

3
It was a quiet summer, the concrete track
Bending down the fields to the pale shore
With no cars parked, no shouting, no one in
Sight but me and the man tending his beach
Barbecue which no one wanted and at length
Sitting motionless staring at the incoming tide.

4
No sound but the beating of waves and the generator
Engine behind the shop chugging away, things
Of residual time worn lightly because
A long past means a sure future and twinned
To the extent beside us is a sense of love
Where centres meet and agree to become unstable.

5
And the Centre of Anything is a Hell of Lack
The Mouth of Which is a Wide Shore
Feeding Generosity into a Rubbish Bin
Called EAT ME: a Country where Each
Has his own Centre and Swells there in the Strength
Of Winning, a Hole as Deep as it is Wide.

6
These Spenserian periods passed before
My mind as I sat there thinking things
I cannot now recall and through my binoculars
Distinctly saw my father in a large winged
Armchair floating on the sea about half
A mile out, heading north and singing Handel,

7
"Gentle Morpheus, son of night…" so like
A winged deity crossing the sun's red core
As it descends to the sea our senses move in
Traverse to the world's pull, that downy peach
That gets us in the end, and surely a strength
Of purpose survives the lapse of will, a sleeper's guide

8
Across the drowsy shore where centuries before
Hundreds landed daily, peasants merchants kings
Barefooted and lost, ghosting the outer rose.
The man in the white coat went and turned
The engine off behind the shop. The lamp above
My head flickered in the wind like a palmer's candle.

VII. Eight Seaside Chapels

1   *St Beuno's at Pistyll*
A place where people can shelter from one dream
In another, the finished dream, the walls hung
With medicinal herbs, the light dim and opaque.
Here you could silence the press and begin to address
Directly the separation of desires. Through thick
Stone walls the fruit trees rattle like the sea.

2   *Llangwnnadl*
Where travellers rest. I sit in the silence,
Doing and thinking nothing for as long
As I can bear it. Triple aisled light in which
I lose my name. But my stomach hurts, my nose
Bleeds, isn't that enough self for today or
Anyone? The lark turns, rest your shadow and belief.

3   *St Merin's Church*
Grassy humps in a clifftop field. A sunset beam
From the sea spreads through the stalks, among
Nettles and cow-parsley faint turf lines, dim shape
Of nave and apse. Here I lay my self crest
To rest, I hope, and crowned commoner O quick-
ly, turn north, where distance makes free.

4   *Bryn Celli Ddu*
Gentle Orpheus, son of light. You are the sense
At the centre, the mechanism through which the long
Beam passes at morning and evening, the bridge
Across the heart in the darkness that grows
Daily finer as the body ages and at the core
Of which a line of light writes final relief.

5   *Llandudwen*
What is that relief? O wait and see, the cream
Of liberty is not to know, the prize is the sung
Response echoing in a stone room the shape
Of a person built over a grave. Cornered. So dress
Your anxious head proudly in the thick
Brightness. Be that engine which learns to be.

6   *Capel Anelog*
And this site of which nothing at all remains
Was where the final question was asked on the long
Pilgrimage to Bardsey. "Did you remember to bring
The tin-opener?" or "Did you really expect the rose
To be an inner answer to unwelcome law, or,
If now is almost time isn't it far too brief?"

7   *Ffynnon Fair*
Now is over, over the hill. The waves scream,
The waves crash. Here on the brown rocks hung
Over nothing, here at the impossible landing, cape
And hood gathered close, distance is set to our best
Sight—for we saw people prepared to stick
To their truth. The island lies before us on the sea.

8
The salt raging within, the ravenous remains
Of the earth running in the vein, reaching the tongue
And bursting into courtesy. An everyday thing,
Far removed from the sickness and errors that bring
Every day of self to a weary and troubled repose.
Far away on the night shore the salt wings close.

VIII. Seawatch

1
Sunk in a grass hollow in the cliff, my station,
A grave green chair. The sea is blue green white,
The sea is grey and folds, the sun is split
And the clouds are a fire. Truth is never
Quite the same, its quantum cracks but
Like a three quarter moon hands down adoring stead.

2
Which is a pulsing certitude a gently
Wavering assurance. The sea throws
Silver coins at the rock. The whimbrel, that shuns
The sight of man, passes down the coast
And a heron follows, for if we are still
We are welcomed, if we are one we are met.

3
A wind up the coast, scent of a milling nation
Traverses the brow so calm a bright
Disposal is for a moment carved a bit
Above his hand and for a fraction the ever
Fractious lark curves over his head. He says I am but
A shepherd of the plain, without ambition, later dead.

4
Stuck in the middle of life, that ungently
Grinds of ruin while the sea is a knife thrown
Across the earth. This evening it darkens
From grey to white and draws at what cost
I don't know the light from the fields until
Swathed in shade I let it go for sixpence net.

5
My O my I thought I had a notion
To validate with truth this brittle
Spending, at every smile and every bite bent
Closer to the ground shifting the weather
Onto my back and wearing like Canute
A crown of clifftop grass and soil all the way to bed.

6
Now it is the middle of night. The empty
Waves continue to knock on the land, down
There. Still some light clings to the sea and the floss
Flickers on the rocks. Human will bearing its star-crossed
Ensign haunts the black interior for good or ill. Spots
Of rain on my coat, are you with me yet?

7
And it will be good. The clouds open: a true equation
Dominates the eastern sky, bright Queen of it:
The shadow of the earth rises across the firmament,
Proving us truly here. And working hard, wherever
Some portion of true hope lies open in the cut
Of a single life (knife, wife, strife, head).

8
When I get back to the caravan it is twenty
To four. Stumbling in the darkness I hear a moan
Of blame, a sleeping urge to die and quit this mess.
But there is no speed at all, no wily ghost.
I tuck the blankets round me heavy with dew,
Closing on sea moon and all, but alive in you.

2

SIX PROSE PIECES

St Merin's church, 7:30 p.m. 2nd October 1977

A chrysalis clinging to a grass stalk. Foundations, lines of shaped stone, green granite sunk into the turf. There was never any final sermon, advice, lesson, instruction – the truth was on its way to the boundary of the sphere and, as it were, intercepted here, and speech was made possible. Marking the ground, leaving a grassy hump in a field with traces of stone edging. The sun gets under the cloud on its way down the sky and will soon settle into the sea, without the hiss heard in heroic times. The peninsula funnelled human souls to a final stadium, of which there is nothing left.

No oracle. You could hardly commit questions to a grassy hillock with a lump where the altar used to be. Answers are not to be expected from a texture of nettles, brambles, and autumn grass stalks. Indeed it is very difficult to live on this earth and you should avoid getting stuck in all funnels except the one that leads to the realisation of hope, the sundering shift to love and its reward. The ground is pitted with holes and people do not know how they got to be where they are; it is fruitful also to forget. Skin tremors on the brink of independence or fight the question-mark back to its cave.

And it doesn't matter, that too will bury itself in time and be forgotten into a monument. A chrysalis on a grass stalk at the west end, sunset out on the sea and within this relic of a purposeful enclosure it becomes feasible to hinge on time as a progressing scan and welcome the faintest chime of reciprocity. We are not alone. Cheep, chirr, whatever is out in the darkness. Faint cries. Populations skimmed by love's edge.

St Merin's church, 7 p.m., 9th September 1978

The wren darts under the thorn and a piece of wind pushes a stinging nettle onto my hand and I hear you as clear as a bronze bell over the sea. We live for what we truly know, slight as it may be, letting go of time in gratefulness. All the green boxes are open and casting their words, a healing scent in the air, a slight recognition, a treatise on what we live for, entirely alone as a few drops of rain patter on my shoulder as if requesting my attention, and strike the open page, and refresh the stinging nettle.

These constantly made and re-made pacts, the gulls flying back to roost through low cloud, the eye sinking down the page in search of the earth's blackness. And a constant distant roar, sea or traffic, what difference would that make? A constant distant roar.

There is no lack of wealth but there is a lack of prosperity. There is no lack of ideas but there is only one thought on the ground tonight, that the person bears a radius beyond the earth, and everything s/he does is the literature of that nation and no other. The crown writes itself into the forehead and the whole structure stands squarely but awkwardly on a disavowal of superior understanding, balanced across the earth on comical tripods. And the thief makes off at dusk with the gain in an understood version, leaping the rocks, ringing the silver bell into hell's mouth. The drops increase, I shelter the page under my mack, where it is already night. The sun's lower orb stands in the pulpit again, the condition is inescapable. He burns in my face across the rain.

We don't add up to what we are, logarithms of grace.

St Merin's churchyard, 7:30 p.m., 9th September 1978

Hurriedly extemporised sermons in long grass are less than half the pilgrim's map, as it gets dark.

Get back to work, however ill you feel, prise the event out of inner sanctity until the ground opens ahead.

Poetry is such a personal thing, but meshing the surface into parcels of time and the edge glitters.

Break these trusts and it is a reign of terror: civil engineers conduce our lives, love is an official secret, ignorance is funny bliss.

The sun bears down on the sea, its royal road a narrow path across the wide sound, constantly changing.

Save us, sun, me, anything in this physical garden, from the automatism we die of, the unbeing we try not to wish.

A spring on the upper slopes of Mynydd Anelog, 11pm 6th September 1979

Stepping out of the bracken into a still circle and all those questions and urgencies mounting up for weeks and weeks disappear. Dry spring, scattered with stalks. As there is no reason to be here, there is no reason to leave, but only to sit in the grass in a circular clearing in bracken and open the mind box to its own ends, free as the wind, to enter that state of children and old people, having all the time in an exact clearing.

Out there the sea is a dreadful confusion of directions with no boundary, horizon washed-out, a grey ghost in the wardrobe of the sky. Here in the image of protection, there is no need for advance.

Then if there were to be in someone's life a direct and "final" questioning or coming to a point, the shelter found under this bright bank says it will always be postponed, as long as there is any working format of hope.

The return to the main road will be a dream manipulation. Up here in the twiggy cirque it is wide awake and slightly chilly but simple and clear as it can't be on waged ground. For anyone, this winning light. The house on the horizon is called Mount Pleasant.

In a white van on the road outside the site of Capel Anelog, 11:40pm 6th September 1979

There can be very little against us except fear. Sometimes we can mend our errors in dream. I had an aged aunt who died when I was thirteen, before I had learned how to make myself welcome to her, though I knew I was a surrogate grandchild.

The sermons are muffled under tufts of yellow grass between slate-roofed stone sheds. Too many questions and no answers. If nothing occurs to you try occurring to someone else.

Push open the door of the dark cottage in the evening, enter softly, feel across the small room to where the old woman sits among her guardian furnitures, nodding half asleep in an arm-chair near the fire, take her hand, rouse her gently and whisper in her ear under the tuft of yellowish white hair, "Hello auntie, it's me, it's your nephew." Forgive her sudden tear, and her pretence: she had forgotten you were coming.

Rhwngyddwyborth, 6th September 1980 in a terrific rush in the middle of packing the car to go

Rusty tramlines carry us into the hell of resentment. To the end of a life signed with a list of dead factories producing nothing but their own smoke. Stupid work, O stupid focus while it is a beautiful morning it really is. O what a beautiful morning as if the sky and planet played bouncy-ball together, played any lived nonsense in bright intellectual ardour... "Put the table out," she says, "Put out the table."

3

POEMS AND NOTES

(1982)

                                              fixed points in
succession, a chain of stations through the land,
a tumulus on a metallic vein, hill fort on a volcanic dome
a processional sequence, that breaks
the disorderly obstructions to desire
and needs constant renewal – a well in the
valley, homestead under the hill, sermons
along the route… grave stone.
Gather up the silver threads in the rubble
that twine together to a gleam in the distance,
the world's treasure at its final section.

So it is from side to side the cloth of gold,
bright and dark with gorse and hawthorn
patchwork of farms and volcanic domes, thick
with fish and wheat and leading somewhere,
to a point, the roads sunken below
head height gathering closer and joining as
the land narrows, pushing towards the distance
or end, the island, the saints'
repose, the logical outcome.

Dithyrambic, after the Vicar of Aberdaron

Death-ray antics
salt fire in the air (sulphur)
      a sacrifice, a nucleus,
a cloth of dust, a nuclear blast
lepers' hospice, cancer chapel –

"No pronoun applies to God" –
          pronouns: circus animals in a field,
moon on snow, close to the sea,
      television (concrete) glow
gardens overgrown in forest spread (cloth of humus)
"a lot of time on one's knees in small churches"
      words lost on the wind –
      absence: traps, warm nests (footprints)
inner emptiness, outer florescence, carved.
      Subcutaneous moth / thorn violin
shadowed field / sea changes / broken cloudbase
brightened field / laser moment / point of departure
peninsular serpent grasps moon-egg
      shells buried in grain.

Ptolemy on Llŷn: *Ganganorum Promontorium* – the Gangani an Irish tribe, and the name Llŷn or Lleyn related etymologically to Leinster.

Rome recognised Llŷn as a separate and distinctive area, a *pagus* (whence French *pays*) – "a natural whole shaped to the purposes of man."

Now "a refuge for monks and pirates".

"The constant glow of light all round the horizon that bespeaks the presence of the sea".

Not through rich fields, but through fields of world to the rich point, is the path of the good man.

(1983)

Late autumn, the peninsula on the turn, about to become the winter-land impossible for foreigners.

Humped shape of Bardsey on the sea, blotted out as another grey rainstorm sweeps over it.

Home, and the small head-glow round it, the working sphere of a life. Occasional lights in the windows of some of the cottages on the headland.

Rain curtain draws over the sea. The bitterness between the object and its image.

Sweeps up towards the mainland over Mynydd Anelog, the bracken curve, the erased chapel, the old woman living in a Nissen hut with about fifteen dachshunds, rope and wire stretched from shed to shed, vibrating in the shout of climate.

Porth Gwrtheyrn, 21st August 1985

Yellow poppy, groundsel, carlin thistle,
Tangles of metal rope, rusted iron cogwheels
Sunk in sand. Slate, granite, aggregate, shale.
Flung wiremesh, rails, bolts, rivets, grills,
Axle, roller, valve, beam, plate.
Rustle of water down cliff-face. Hawk, goat,
Wild shore strewn with lumps of concrete.
Mermaid's purse, crab-shell, sandhoppers, boat.
Plastic bottles, rope knots, tin cans, bird bones.
Oystercatcher, little gull, wave smacks gravel.
My hair a thin cushion against the stones.
Concrete telegraph hut, bits of copper cable
Still dangling from it. Monster ruin of loading quays.
My family, my lunch, my erratic, growling days.

A Repetition of Machado at Porth Gwrtheyrn

The soul creates its own shoreline.

Mountains of ash and lead.

Little arbours of spring.

Porth y Nant

Exposed slate beds on the road down to the deserted village, grained vertically, blades upwards to the feet, and slippery where little water-courses spill onto the road.

Vast bent shore, heavy brown gravel crunched under the long waves.

Derelict machine-buildings in the cliff, bracken and bushes on decayed concrete terraces, big iron cog wheel half-buried in the shore.

Part of a wooden pier thrust into the sea from a concrete filtering-shed, sea pebbles falling out of concrete walls, shreds of corrugated iron, lichen, sea mulch, encrusted strips of copper wire lying on the shingle outside the roofless telegraph shed.

Wild goats on the cliff terraces, among the stone chutes.

One of the "ends of the earth". Passages to something else, something not-earth? A new language? A moneyless economy? Remote unvisited stretches of shore where people gather to launch themselves on the sea in bids of escape, in frail home-made boats hoping to avoid the eyes of coast guards and storms. Victims of other people's wealth. Desperate prayers, overheard by the sea.

4

SEA WATCH OVERSTOCK

1. Pieces, fragments, and notes during the writing of Sea Watches 1984-7

* * *

So calm and clear a day you could turn and face it,
and say, "My life is a mince of pain."

An earth tremor, a low rumble, the little grocery shop
at Rhydlios trembles and the tins rattle on the shelf
we thought a heavy goods vehicle had passed by.

The farm: earthen banks separate the fields, the fields
scattered with goose feathers dung and mushroom stalks
to the cliff edge, furrows of white rock.

Hollow bone, porous tuff, delicately poised at the land's edge
an industrialist's wink could crush all of it

Except the calm clear factor
spoken trembling in florescent stone.

* * *

Insane hilltop citadels on igneous outcrops
heather filling the air with sweetness, stonechats perched
on swaying bracken fronds, patches of broken stone

sphagnum grasses, bilberry, insane citadels guarding
nothing, ravings of old men, actor-politicians,
the body preserved and guarded in the mountain-top house
pride of intellect spasm of power

but wishes all shall fail thee.

* * *

Crossville Bus Company, Pwllheli 2458 or Caernarfon 4631
Route Llangwnadl–Nefyn. No go the circus.
Telephone box vandalised. A fritillary at St Mary's Well.

Buzzed by a RAF jet from Anglesey, the herd runs towards
    the sea.
Enter a bald woman leading a blind child.
"The world can only be served by the extraordinary" (Goethe)

* * *

Walking in the dark night, sea sky and land
confused together. Noisy sea. Dim, clouded flickering
of house windows... again an earth tremor.

>Nothing but the total gimpsed in facets
>and so the fish eyes in the tree
>the cars honking each other
>the ground thick with crossed bone.

Phil Davenport died this week in Mozambique.

No return, a single light ahead across the cancelled fields.

* * *

Waking in the night
I see the door-light through your hair.

* * *

A faint cry in the night, of sandpipers
through the steady wind and rain on the roof

>"brine stings the window" (B.C.)

The faint piping of oyster-catchers in the morning
like an aeolian machine behind the steady
rain on the roof and the wind on the corners.

Collect these details, as your wages.

2. The Nightwatch Notebook

Texts prepared in 1989 for Sea Watches VIII, *then called "Eight Sea Sunsets" and the whole work "Shining Cloth", written at night out on the cliff or on returning to the caravan, in either case in the dark and not entirely legible.*

A. Saturday   [In manus tuas

Between insistence and response a sudden crack
a report of unknown origin
three-quarter moon low over the farmhouse.
Imperfect circle, perfect fear.

Saturday (2)   [de Sermisy's Lamentations

The world-sheet folding the line through time
as the arm turns inward for protection
against the spread [? against the speed]

A land hump black against the silver turmoil
that advances greedily but wants no reward,
a long stone against the star, a theory that works
that predicts reliably and declares its limits
and opens the door for the singers.

Sunday

Cloudy complicated sunset, patches and layers shifting
against each other on the horizon, a dark underlay
moving gently from left to right, family of three choughs
on the headland, their hollow cries
Sitting so still "a god might enter him"
Sitting so still an equation might settle on his arm.
[...]
Patchwork of yellow cloud-wisps carpeting the sky.
Like a night watchman his freedom

disperses into echo, a proof might
pass through him [...]

C.   [Lassus, Byrd

Cirque of rain clouds. What did we see today?
A wet moth clinging to a grass stalk.
An ancient church in a clump of elms.
Dark grey turbulent sea pounding the land, you
cannot love it "To love the sea is only
to love death" (Mann) Still head
Still head in the passage of weather
A wet moth clinging to a grass stalk.

D   [Hildegard

Light is torn from us.

To end up alone in a grim seaside bungalow
(homo fragilis) smelling slightly unsavoury
and burning the night light as the spray
hits the window in outer dark, harbour [?harvest]
of the extraordinary, eyes turned back in.

The horizon blurs, a flock of jackdaws black rags
against the sky, waiting, the dark will come in
and the light will go out, the light will be restored.

The strange animals in the head will dine together.

E   [Taverner
(Eclipse of the Moon: 17th August 1989, 2:30 a.m.)

Never stop. Pause and protract. Withdraw
and separate. Lay items together in order

like a stone wall on top of a cliff, a spider's web
across a culvert. Listening for an answer.
"Death should not be a problem. If all goes well,
you pass into dreaming and the world vanishes."

Waves, wing-beats.

[F and G are lost except for one word, "lucifer" or possibly "dulcimer"]

H

Back at the caravan I switch the light on to a chorus of complaints.
I make myself some cocoa and read Chinese poems.
The "I" of these poems is always alone.

* * *

Soul tangled in wires [?violas]
serious, uneven, alone, not-alone,
worried about the gas cylinder
the fire that flowers at the end of breath

Worrying florescence that might
suddenly go pop. And the head fire
fall into dream leaving everything unfinished.
A string band playing in the farmyard in the middle of the night?

* * *

Later the blur intensifies, moon over a black shed
glows like a light bulb through ice
thin strips of cloud in streaks across sky
like something very fast photographed
but there is no speed. Waiting to pass
into company.

* * *

I settle comfortably into bed
by the small caravan window
onto grey field edge, black shed
and streaks across the sky. Legible,
heartening lines. Too dark to
write, I write. I fill the pages.

*　*　*

Filtered moonlight on the bed,
serious words, some of them,
about nothing much, the head of a tree
against the sky, a wish for sleep,
serious breathing in the room, like a lighthouse.

*　*　*

And so calm and clear the shining cloth
curvature of [?thought] which
passes, becomes cloudy, spreads
into a width of mental movement
also in [   ] of largesse for
tomorrow, [   ]ing what we keep
when we lose the moon and the sea and the whole
[two lines written on top of each other]
saves terrestrial events from waste.

5

Mornings with a Walkman at Rhwyngyddwyborth
(1989-90)

Never relenting creation of event, at the still point
in the world sheet, the whirling sheet.

Butterflies: blue, white, yellow-white, pale brown,
dry thrift tenacious to the stone,
lichens: orange, white, cream-brown.

The city occluded in distance
but speaking clearly on a good wire.

A tern plummets to the sea and curves back
at the good moment / a cormorant hangs
on the meniscus and slides into the music.

Their rate of expenditure is low: we need them.
A whole flock of whimbrel.

Sea wind across his voice,
a paralysed man in a wheelchair on the sea-front at Llandudno
requests the Eroica,
all of it,
and insists on period instruments.

* * * * * * *

And all calm, all clear, crisp, all Cs.
Nothing can take this light,
passed on, generation to generation
it is everywhere.
And to bear it, to take it in hand
we make it a dark light
a light spread over
the dull gleaming acres of sea shifting
this way and that, a constant light
worked through the dark seething land
forking and crossing and burning at points
in living rooms and supermarkets
the light the line the lineament of love
longing for its lost spaces, the departed air.

* * * * * * *

A bush full of sparrows.
Spearmint by the roadside.
Small flocks of oystercatchers and one curlew, disturbed on
    the cliff top.
Martins round the black barn.
Dark cloud band dark sea, circled in light.
Ink sea.
Cloud band breaks at edges, grey theatre.
A light moving on the sea.
The farmer has died and his boat lies in its shed all summer.
Pleasure boats edge into the cove and sail away.
Gorse bushes clicking in the heat.
Massed clouds over the mainland.
If you abhor privacy, you abhor history.
Wrest the emptiness to the bone, play knucklebones with it.
Peace exists as an inner turmoil.
Two families of choughs on the cliffs.
How many more years, this holiday?
I get heavy and toil up hills.
Events are repeated a tone lower each year [cantus firmus].
Corrugated sky, thickening towards the horizon, stretching
    beyond sight, streaked with light.
Cliff edge walks. Little flocks of passerines, the ordinary folk of
    these demesnes.
Clear pools in the rocks, gently rising and falling.
To be engaged with the world, from the house onwards
    – strictly in that direction, kindly.
On all our queries and requests for assurance the world
    maintains graceful impermeability
which keeps us going, year after year.

Things Saying Themselves in Llŷn

Late evening at the caravan. Very quiet, slight wind in the bushes outside, darkening, faint plash and grind of sea beyond the field. I finish a bottle of rosé with some herb-flavoured Welsh goats'-milk cheese, which I take with a small coffee-spoon from a sheet of foil spread on a saucer. It signifies nothing, waiting to be written-over and replaced, as we work a life through in the earth's terms and are replaced. The earth continues, the sea keeps on breaking on the shore for centuries with hardly a shift of tone, storms come and go, the calm clock-like breaking continues. As everyone knows. I was fifty last week. Grey hairs dominate my headscape. I move slower over the cliff paths. Inwardly I am still that scowling child in the photograph, wanting to know what keeps it from the world, deeply resenting the tension between bosom and horizon. I sit in a corner and scowl at all the light and horror that passes the window. It is a relief when the evening wraps all that away and settles like a blanket over the earth, and the sullen child reaches his rest: there is really nothing out there you need to know, but gently whispering grass and a white sonorous border where the land falls to the sea. For the moment tenable, held in trust for tomorrow and another puzzled, resentful infant being shown the sea and told to make the best of it. To return at fifty to the same distant coast, cleared at last of guardians.

(a) We climb Carn Fadrun and picnic on the curved ledge near the top among heather and stones and bilberry. A palomino pony comes over to share our lunch. Then we walk over to the area under the crest, sheltered from the wind, and stumble around awkwardly on the broken surface, tracing prehistoric hut circles and eating the bilberries. The children play at "estate agents" and sell the hut circles to each other.

(b) We visit the north corner of Hell's Mouth at low tide and stroll slowly among rock pools and mussel beds, turning over stones here and there to note shore crabs, hoppers, and shrimps. We move stones and clumps of seaweed to divert the course of a small sand-stream. There's no one else in the entire vast stretch of bay, hazy with spray coming landward. I notice a cave some thirty yards up a small black cliff with water coming out of it and falling to the shore. I climb up to it and find it's an old mine adit, which I enter and follow in for about 20 yards where it ends in a small black pool, probably hundreds of feet deep.

(c) I walk round Mynydd Carreg looking for pieces of jasper in the long grass of the old quarries.

(d) We buy a bottle of goats' milk from the two old women who live in the white cottage in the fields at Rhydlios. A small house standing in the middle of a collection of structures which have accrued to it over the years – two caravans, various sheds, pens and paddocks, kennels, fruit trees, a veranda, and a long earthen mound with goat bones sticking out of it.

(e) We walk over Uwchmynydd towards the sea in the early afternoon. It's a very dry summer, the slopes grey and brown with thin grass, the tracks baked hard. It would be very hot but for the constant sea-wind. The vegetation on seaside fells is always stunted, clings to the ground, constantly halted by wind and salt: low firm heather patches vibrating in the wind, gorse bushes clenched and bent. Dust falls from the ground as our feet break it at stony lips. We walk over the dome and down a small valley towards St Mary's Well, the slope increasing as we descend. We mount the far side a little, and stop to sit on a small rock outcrop and have our lunch. There's just enough space. Opposite us a National Trust warden is strimming a patch of bracken near the site of St Mary's chapel. Why is he doing this? Why should any person or institution ever want to strim bracken on an open hillside? In the base of the cleft below us are two wheatears moving around on the path, foraging and returning. Then we walk down towards the sea, a huge blue plane tilted towards us, Bardsey Island riding it in the middle distance like a roosting seal. We mount to the right onto the lip of the cleft and out onto the cliff shoulder hanging over the sea, then down the stone steps hewn at some time, by someone, in the granite cliff and finally onto a pile of rocks at the edge of the sea. This is where the well is, round a corner to the right, a long stoup on the cliff face in a lichened crevice with fresh water dripping into it and trickling out at the other end. One by one we creep along the rock ledge over the breaking waves to reach the spring. One by one we scoop up the water in a green plastic cup and drink it.

6

SEA WATCH ELEGIES

The world-sheet breaks time open
We are the waste some of which gets called back
Curved back to surround random events like
A shell and offer the future a site
A line that stands a long stone
Against the star a trust that opens
At its point – we are set again we are
Daily beings, yearly ideas, we stick.
The silver turmoil warns and arms us,
Passing home.

Δ

Cloud-sheet lit from below
Orange bands
Wind in grass
A man walking on the cliff
Passing measures
Serrated perspectives
Accumulated lives
Replaced persons
Measured thoughts
Choired land.

Δ

Like a night-watchman over the sea
A shepherd of the plain, not without ambition, I
Stay, still enough for the balance to rest its
Question here.

Cirque of rain clouds to the west
A wet moth clinging to a grass stalk
Questioning welcome

Dark grey, turbulent sea, flecked waste,
Quick moving air on the cheek
Hater of governments, lover of order

World order – Answer it, this
Mindless power. There is nothing to stop us
Loving in peace and constancy.

To end up alone in a grey house
Grim grey seaside bungalow
A few gathered belongings
Persisting with a work
Of uncertain provenance or future
Dark wine in the evening
A collection of tapes
Without you I am nothing,
A leaf in the wind an old fox
Walking unhurriedly to earth.

Δ

Black rags cast in the
Grey sky, light infused
With meaning
Meaning take your stick and go
Everything is busy without you
And so he does
To a room, and lights a lamp.

Waves noises through the walls
Black scraps cast on a page
Defying passage.

Δ

Alone in the house
A green shelf over the sea
The few things needed
Work to be done
Certain and necessary
Dark wine in the evening
Various musics
Always with you
Wherever you are
Set on earth.

Waves (dim things) pushing at the land
All night through the thick walls
Begging, thoughtless begging
Suddenly stops and we agree
We agree to live in a world
To live in a world
That does have worldness.

Δ

"As he lived so he died,
In mild and quiet sort"

Like a night watchman or a
Welsh farmer steadily

Binding the fences
Calming the afflicted

And his belief
In worldness

Leaving me alone or worldless
Up here on the cliff top at night
Everyone asleep behind me
Stop pushing, roll over.

Δ

Two hundred and forty-fifth wave
Rolls over, two hundred and forty-sixth
Everyone busy elsewhere as I
Watch nothing on purpose
And worth every second too, as the vast
Haul of dark earths our core.

Δ

Night winds hugging the coast
And night birds sailing
Over the ground-light, over the sea.

One lit window, over there, along the cliffs
Attending day. Let me
Too be nothing but

Δ

And never stop,
Lay the pale stones together
On the edge of the land
That warn the traffic and
Shepherd the stray

Thoughts to their purpose.
Set aside a tenth of the profit
For the commonalty.

And at last, pale streaks across the sky
Thin cloud televising dawn
Ice crystals
Float over the house
And black shed.

Δ

The grass again.

Δ

Always saying more
There is no more to say
But to beg release and
Order it down: world go
Under, go under world.
For we hate it. We've
Had enough. Enough world
Enough wine. Enough cold/hope.

Δ

And creep into bed at last
Into darkness in the day
And peace and closure in the plains of loss.
And the pains of lessness fall.

7

THE TRANSLATIONS OF
ST COLUMBA'S SEA-WATCH

1.
To be enfolded bodily in a summit
Like the ink in a letter
And witness the sea's entire calm.

2.
The heaving waves riding the glitter
A continual singing
Addressed to a cause.

3.
The clear headland with its smooth strand
We are established at the outer edge
Cloaked in brightness, smeared in birdsong.

4.
The local waves beating on the rocks
The [—]¹ from the graveyard.

5.
Great flocks of birds hanging over the sea
Rare mammals² passing down the coast
Gods of food, gods of want, human centres.

6.
Watching the tide rising and falling, my
Back to the land, I attain my secret name.

7.
And recognise my failings, so difficult to speak out.
A contrite or empty heart, watching the sea.

8.
Honour the movers of these powers:
Sky messengers, earth cakes, ebb and flow.

9.
Read books good for the soul.
Learn to avoid power of lies.
Meditate silently, sing aloud.

10.
I gather dulse from the rocks, I go fishing
I share the food in the community
Alone in my room.

11.
So to think further the simple heights of physics
That redeem our term, and the necessities become
Lighter, and life is [prized.]³

---

¹ *possibly* shout, call
² *glossed* whales
³ *query* priced *or* prised

8

Overheard by the Sea

— an abandoned poem —

Earth rises to the foreplain between love and understanding.
It takes the gull path, you can almost feel the tremble,
The surrender, the flare of passage. How can we wait here,
How can we not be there where the waves break on the horizon
To announce a new island? Pains of guilt, end pasture,
Falcon's lunch, how can I escape uncaring if the song
Returns to first base, how do you spell excise? Fields fall
To the sides of the sky like words in transit to a new tongue
In the hope of the townships. Vast bay, sea hauling gravel
Like a thousand typists bone to metal, wheel against
Wheel at the land's edge our lives are milled out:
All we have left, pushed against earth's lock.

Earth light cast into the sky over the sea,
Raised in a hand that arches back to home, and where
Is it now, the faithful turf, a fractured line in the sky,
The whole massif plunging westward into sunset.
We lose what we want and get what we are: a coat to wear,
"woven of thorns and nettle stems" someone
Shall no doubt wear us for a while against the death
Of socialism like a shadow on the skin.

Home is cancelled. Home is a green caravan tucked
Into a corner of a wheat field, its windows
Glowing dimly as evening drains the day. A lost
Photograph blown over the pier railing, the nation
As it might have been; we set down to the arts
Of survival, tend our scattered fires in clefts of the
Coastal rocks as if waiting for a transport, and what
Was that noise? What was that sudden planet-like rasp?
The tall grasses still hold the light and the ruined cottages
Glow in the evening, the tick of a heart, "a small cell
Among many graves…" and the heart knows, the boat
Will be in one day and a bonny boat swift with the tide,
Set for the harbour lights / sons and daughters, factors
Of the receding pulse am I there in that treatise did I win a
        place
In the log of love? You lovesick sailors I wanna go home.

9
BETWEEN HARBOURS

1

Long and tiring journey
through car zones

Arrive "washed out"
back of neck, eyelids, shoulders

Walk down to the sea, where
metal stays sheathed.

All the stones are rounded
and form sentences together it

Doesn't matter what you hate and drink it
matters what the heart answers dying dying.

2

It matters when, the heart questions,
dying to finalise these taunting distances

And be where you live. A wild home
or a protecting distance, where

The stones beat against the sea
growling and grinding together to form

A musical sentience, darkening as the
earth turns and the gulls descend.

Wine, supper, silence and sleep. The stones say
every breath is kept safe to the end.

3

In the little cove the stones rattle and squeak,
a thin stream comes down to the sea and the
slight waves tonight tap idly on the rocks.

My night camera, favourite spot, journey's end.
Between driven earth and halting sea
the tide like a little washerwoman scrubs

The pebbles smooth and grades them in strata
and with Beckettian astringency repeats
what little she knows every eight seconds.

Further out the real sea, a vast self a vast unit
that pulls away from time and sorrow and knows
only its own sense, and picks at the shore

As at the edges of an itchy scab. Its own hero,
its own journey its own faint curiosity at
otherness and love. I walk back up the cove

To the fence that separates all this from
the possible, and traverse it at a 5-barred gate,
waking the farm dogs. I head for the small

Window-light across a vast indigo haze
belonging only to the world, pebbles
in my pockets, arguing about the waste of days.

4

The sea seems to breathe slowly, and to fall
one step at a time, because the universe

Is what it is, calling and calling and calling,
attracting everything to its path, death.

A red mullet falls out of it and I
slit it with a sharp knife avoiding

The poisonous spikes, setting aside
the blue liver and shiny bowels.

I make rather a mess of it, failing to clear
the smallest bones, but it makes a good meal

Eaten with care, with world trust
under the conflicting messages.

5

A few minutes on the shore, in the small cove
the body complaining as the stones roll

And shift underfoot and the substance
of the sea changes with the light.

Lies told proudly by the Thames change the sound
the sea makes on a small Welsh shore

More than they change the welcome behind
the lit window. Something more than the earth,

Some priority, cuts the haze and clears
the difficult ground the failing

Body tracks to the end. Head wobbling
on top of it saying I've lost my watch.

6

A figure standing on the little shore like a statue
a post sunk into the shingle as night slowly falls
the noise of breaking fills the air and little

Wave rims ply around his shoes. All the white lines
and pale fences of dark England snaking through
his body as he stands there like a notice board

At the water's edge, all the roads and service stations
of his way there abseiling down his digestive system
like the belly-dance down a Cimabue crucifix from panel

To panel to the end, the foot, the fixed point on which
the horizon spins into reverse and the midnight special
shines its ever-loving light on me.

7

The length of anyone's life, a gathering of traces,
dim ghosts on the dark surface of memory swaying
from side to side like a boat coming quietly to harbour
crunching on the stones and stopping.

To bring back what is gained, to climb the steep
track up the cove the sea growling below and the wind
combing my hair I smile back and head for
something less permanent, and much more clear.

Back the twisty path up the cliff to the headland,
and cross the dim field towards a known condition
and a short time, that sees a long way and is
over before you know it, I can't wait.

To deny eternity and lie under blankets between
thin walls while the gas cylinder growls and,
asked the question, answer Yes: this brevity,
and separation, is what I came here for.

8

Red gas-fire glow, dark space, blankets firm on
cheek and shoulder, slight wind noise outside

And that thing standing down there on the shore
like a life-belt holder, scratched and marked

With the colours of earth, full of
twisting cloud and longing for peace,

By the water's edge where probably the first life
on earth floated idly towards the stones

Or gods and goddesses from the curvature of the earth
rode to shore in a wooden boat called Absolute Certainty

And met a notice saying Welcome. No Parking. Pay
at the kiosk. And saw a waterfall twisting down the cliff

An old man warming his hands at an electric fire
and a list of indulgences pinned to a door, which opens

And I wake up in earth's brightness. Smoke
rising from the harbour, wet grass, hunger.

10

SIX SMALL PROSE PIECES
FORMERLY ATTACHED TO
BETWEEN HARBOURS

1
Noticing the Holyhead lighthouse several miles away across the fuzz and remembering a wet evening at Dalkey, strolling among the captains' retreats, thick-walled one-storey houses set at angles among the coastal rocks, after staying too long in the Queen's Bar, when a strange little crowd gathered at Forty Foot because a body was lost. A diver's foot trapped in some old netting on the sea floor. The poets declare how their big souls despise safety.

2
And, three years later, a night in Bray Head Hotel, vast stack of corridors and disused ballrooms with one small person in charge and a woman screaming on the first floor, screaming and howling in drink and rage. The sea won them all in the end, the adventurers and swashbuckling poets, the patient inquirers and victims in despair, grinding against each other.

3
It became a habit on the way back to stop at Llangollen, where a Hungarian immigrant has filled an old cinema with about forty thousand unwanted books. This also is the earth, this theatre of shelving, with its prices, categories, attached tea-shop. Some people have a forward mania, which drives them into the big boss role and everything costs the earth. We should be grateful when it operates small-scale. Later we found a way of avoiding Llangollen.

4
Battles are lost and won in border-zones but creation takes place at the centre, at the peace at the centre, that is what I think. I don't care if I never think anything else in the world.

5
Long reaches of late sunlight on the narrow land, catching the western walls of white houses scattered on a territorial

grid that suddenly stops at the cliff's edge. And the edge runs round the headland alive with dozing boats, white birds, children shouting. The inner edge of what we don't inhabit, and can't know. It promotes contentment, yearning, ice-cream, and soul inflation but look how the long land reaches out to be cancelled.

6

I left the car on the top of the mountain and walked across to Llanllawen, where an old woman lives in a group of three tin huts with about thirty dachshunds. She was cheerful as I passed her perimeter fence, though moving slowly. The dachshunds were an over-excited infant class. Darkness was falling on her enclosure, and the lines joining the tops of her huts, for hanging out washing or bringing electricity, wrote on the paling sky, "There is one true purpose."

11

ABSENT FROM LLŶN

(1994-1997)

4 PROSE POEMS

1.

Four years pass, we don't go there. The little girl we carried across the shore packs a rucksack and goes to Zimbabwe, we don't expect to see her for at least a year.

At the airport she says, "Well, I've had my adventure now, I think I'll go back home" and almost means it, but the plane accelerates into plane zones, and the bird has flown.

Meanwhile, a small cove on the Welsh coast in the night, the sea grinding stones in the darkness, the disused boat sinking deeper into the shingle year after year.

And far from all that distance, in the waiting fulcrum we call home, a smile of trust mounts from the heart like someone climbing a cliff-path, casting knowing eyes on the connecting and severing sea.

2.

The day after Gatwick we take a strange room in Southwold, a loft over a garage with old wooden furniture and a long window-set. It rains a lot, we wander the marshes bereft, our thoughts elsewhere.

And tear drops fall into a mug of instant coffee. But the urgent question is: did I get the message across? Daughter's gone away, before she left did I remember to tell her my story, whatever it is?

When all the pantomime is set aside, all the poetry, did I get round to mentioning the straight message which is all I have in the world, the one thing I know? What in the world is it?

Walking paths through the coastal marshes in the rain, the wet sedge brushing against us as we pass; and always before us that sadly unspeakable certainty, absolutely clear, that takes the best of anyone away from what they are.

3.

Another Christmas card from "All at Rhwyngyddwyborth."

Daughter and wife gone to Egypt. I stay and feed the cats, living alone in the small house that developed round us.

More mysterious symptoms, spinning head, aches behind the knees… Carefully preparing sautéed vegetables in the late evening…

Woke up this morning with an awful aching head, never knew the distance, never solved the far shore blues.

4.

That place there, that anchorage, its tough grass its sparkling rocks, that holds us scattered souls to a focus

And means death too, means succession, somebody's noisy grandchildren on the beach. Life is particularly insubstantial there, it flits across the landscape, a figure on the cliff-top, next moment gone. Restless, reaching sea.

Herring gulls, whimbrels, and choughs, and the small birds that flutter on the fences, riding the wind.

*

The same wind curves across the land, anticyclonic, flicking the last leaves of last year's autumn from the treetops in Cambridge, but stronger straight off the sea, out there. Crows, curlews and herring gulls, soaring down the cliffs as night comes — better than any aeroplane, landing on the nest, calling in the green dark.

And the small birds asleep in the bushes and hedgerows, balanced on one leg, head tucked under wing, asleep but still focused on each other, as the wind shakes the branches, asleep but aware.

*

Aware of distance, aware of poverty, aware of hopelessness, sleeping in identity, one eye half open.

Goodnight from me here with my wine and my word processor, to the green dark out there, full of calls.

12

Llŷn in the Rain
Only the Song

1) Over two mountain passes to meet up with Barny at Blenau Ffestiniog station. Already it's raining. *For Sale* signs all over the town. I think we have uncovered the depopulating source of the eastern England house-price boom. Indeed Barny's been round the town's estate agents pretending to be interested in properties, and says they're almost being given away. But who wants to buy a corner shop for ten thousand, live here surrounded by dereliction and go barking mad in a town with a miniature railway running through its centre? Old slate quarries hovering over the houses, the books in the bookshop all damp, the tired pastries in the bakers' windows. Later we learn how these places return to their identity in bad weather, but as yet it is dull and depressing. We get through to Mrs Jones from a 'phone box: yes, it's all right to go straight there and arrive a day early. We do the supermarket shopping and drive off, plunging behind the town into the granite vale that opens down into Cardigan Bay at Porthmadog.

> Rock and fibre glowing wet, brown and green,
> estuarine light blue under trees:
> a bright line beside us -- we fall between,
> buying the future an earthen dream.

2) A take-away curry from the Tandoori at Pwllheli, which is a whitewashed brick shed just off the sad white rain-washed sea-front, across the road from a boarded-up beer-hall. Sit there waiting for it, nodding at the staff: young Asians living out here, so far from the city communities, I wonder what that feels like. Run through the rain to the car with the wrapped curry and drive on. And when we get to the caravan a shock as we come over the rise towards the farm--it's a new caravan! this is the third. The curry just about warm enough to eat by the time we arrive, but barely curry at all, a strangely sweet stew, which must be what is expected in far west Wales... but we're here. We're all here again.

> Solid cloud into the distance / sea blue-white
> black-tipped waves / threading back to us
> all here all busy / reeling up night
> and small in the rain / trading histories.

3) Mrs Jones had a heart-attack but has been all right since. So she tells us, in that cool matter-of-fact Welsh style as if talking about the price of margarine. In exactly this tone she told us of her brother Goronwy's death from throat cancer eight years ago; who had been our tutor here, shyly greeting us every year, tending our spaces, naming the rocks, taking us out in the boat. No more boat. The fishing is all finished. Licences have become so expensive for the one-boat farmer they have all stopped and their boats rot in coves. Government income from sport fishing, the sea reserved for the boys playing captains. Also Mr Jones (up the road, no relation) has died: said to have been the last man who knew how to make Aberdaron-style wicker lobster-pots. Later we look at his small, tight, weather-proofed house and peer through the windows. The little triangular lawn with tall banks round it, the shed with the pots hanging up. Who will buy it? Young people don't want to live here any more: the '60s pastoral dream collapsed before the new hard domestic economy and its inhering conformism; the rich want their extra houses abroad; the locals have had enough: fishing prohibited, no use farming, sheep two a penny. House prices have not fallen, but they might.

> Raging apart the need and the cost
> hollow distances where the gull sits
> and laughs and the tides roar back
> small change wash hands take it.

And she gives us tea, and tells us where the food shop is this year (for every year the food shop is in a different place) and says how the child has grown as she always does. Mrs Jones who continues year after year while grandparents, parents, brother and neighbour vanish into the landscape.

4) Days of persistent rain. Reading books or playing chess as it beats on the metal walls. It's been like this all summer, and by September no one around at all. I've never seen the place like this. Porth Or a big empty bay, the shop almost abandoned: two young girls in charge of a few racks of leftovers, you can't even get a cup of tea. And everywhere you

go the same quietness, raining or soon will be, Aberdaron, Nefyn, Abersoch — a few stragglers in macks passing from newsagent to grocery store and hurrying back to the car.

I remember going on holiday with my parents to places like Llandudno and Rhyl, and in those days you stayed in boarding houses which gave you breakfast and chucked you out; you weren't allowed to return until the evening meal at six. So if it rained for the week you'd had it, you stared at the shop windows for as long as you could, you lingered in tea-rooms and amusement arcades but basically you sat in the lee-sides of the sea-front shelters. You sat on a bench with half a roof over you wrapped in coats and watched the barren sea frothing or the shops opposite and the battered tulips inbetween until it was time to go back. And this was people's only holiday, they worked 50 weeks of the year in factories offices and shops and this was their one annual break from it. And they spent it sitting in the wind and the rain while the kids sulked and sucked sweets and cried.

But now it's a victory, a restoration. The rubber dragons sitting unsellable in the corner novelty shop while the sea wind shakes the glass door, the guides to Celtica Mystica and works of the previous vicar dampening on the shelves, the watercolours unlooked-at, the candy-floss machine unplugged, the luminous pinks and yellows deflated. It is such a relief, that the place stands so solidly there while the season's sordidities shrivel away. Places arisen for an economic purpose and a spiritual relief, turned into nonsense depositories. And thank God it rains and rains until you think it can't rain any more and then it rains again and the truth finally unwinds: there is actually no reason to come here.

We dart about in this unreason. We nip in and out. We sit with the shore expanse before us through the window of the hotel bar in Aberdaron, the rolling waves washing the brown sand and the standard beer in the glass. We pause before the slate tombstones the biggest crowd seen in these parts for some time. Tea and Welsh pancakes at Carreg Plâs under Mynydd Carreg, surrounded by people talking Welsh. Superb little salty-sweet buttery mouthfuls, and no English worker-snobs spreading their ignorance in the air, their paid-for-it-and-entitled, their contempt for the locals and the language. Outside, rain sweeping the fields and no one on the paths. Bareness over all this peninsula, but native, speaking softly to itself of the music it lacks.

Because an alien centrality took it away and replaced it with a trade in fakes which, predictably, let everyone down when fortune's pink smile faded in the slowing of the gulf stream. Fair-weather traders, find something to sell that people need.

And the wind on top of Uwchmynydd is magnificent, you can hardly stand up in it. The concrete road curls up to the top, you get out of the car and whirl round and the door slams, it blasts across your ears, it hisses round the corners of the coast-guard shed (closed) information centre, the heather tight to the ground vibrating in its passage and you push through it coat flapping to the top of the slope to see Bardsey before you, riding the turbulent ocean two miles off. How the true locations are still there in all the changes of weather and the prosperity badges ripped off, how the sites were made solid enough to pass by all that, and the structures that talk us into it. And us ourselves, certainly.

> Viewing the green theatre behind the rain
> knowing our little cares will increase
> year by year and the red of the petal
> and the red of the fire do nothing but gain.

And no, we shan't get to Bardsey this year either, clearly, but the time will come. The space between it and us is too full. Like the space between prosperity and purpose, full of all that weather and most of what we are, and the silence when everyone's gone away.

> Then green takes its fair shine.
> We wondering what we need
> freely twine red thread on
> walking stick maybe the last time.

5) Porth y Nant under rain, the deserted village rebuilt as a Welsh language centre, and with a café, which even has a few people in it, staring out at wet slopes through steamed-up window, macks dripping onto floor. Signs have sprouted everywhere: *For Sale* in the towns, *Keep Off* at the edges of the land, and there is no one to keep off, and nothing to keep them off. *Private* in front of a bracken-coated cliff, and big red *Danger/Keep Out* all over the remains of the gravel works on the shore and the quarries further on. Institutions protecting themselves from claims, worried before the privatisation of law, plastering warning messages on everything in sight.

Later walking alone up the cliff steps at the south end of the bay because I want to photograph an old farmhouse I remember on the top pastures, the rain really comes on. The stone steps in the cliff, which the workers made for themselves to get down to the gravel loading bays, are little cascades. On the top the wind drives the rain hard against me from landward, it soaks my trouser legs and gets down my neck front and back and into my shoes. I pass that strange wooden dwelling like a cricket pavilion which I'd almost forgotten, and which does look lived-in, but the stone house is silent as ever, sitting there on a shelf of the sloping pastures. Standard Welsh thick-walled small farmhouse, two storey with central porch and slate roof, furnished and curtained but never anyone there, exactly the same for twenty years. So whoever owns it remains elsewhere, and the fact that it's one of the few houses without a *For Sale* sign means they at least survive, whatever they are for good or ill they haven't been dispersed or eradicated by death and change. I stand in front of a house which is a kind of sign saying "We continue" and take a photograph of it. These things are rare. The histories we trade are mostly small change.

And walk behind it across the fields to the cliff top and back down the diagonal path across the face, another workers' route, to the north end of the bay again. Stone sills over red mud. A buzzard hovering over the cliffs, and two choughs on the beams of the derelict quarry house. A mountain goat noticed high up the cliff through the café windows. A lot of seals around, one usually appears whenever we get down to the sea, and two regulars in the left cove at the farm. People move out, but other things move in.

> Rooks circling the green pastures spotted
> with bright red flowers / Are you our ghosts,
> will you protect us? / Future love in the hands
> of black armies, and wandering hosts.

6) Let the rain do its worst, we perform the whole routine, we shirk none of it. We do the full Morfa Nefyn sequence first established circa 1983: drive there along the coastal tract south of Nefyn, which is one of my strongest images of this terrain: the land coming down from the central ridge and striped with stone-walled fields rebounding in a gentle wave before stopping suddenly at the cliff edge – a great scroll of land up the coast. Then get the fish and chips (the F&C shop itself is for sale! this really could be the last time) and take them down to the shore to eat on the rocks, dump the paper in the same green oilcan provided for such purpose for the last fifteen years and then walk over the wetness a mile to Porth Dinllaen. Low tide, we pass close under the stilt houses, some of them showing signs of habitation, mostly not. And the quietness that's everywhere has settled here too: no one in the pub or outside it. Then walk on, the little shore-side path along the edge of the headland. The wooden hut in the cliff niche, still there, someone still getting there maybe a week a year and keeping it going, bottle of washing-up liquid on window-ledge. Somehow people keeping a few things going as desertion settles round them like rain. And on past the lifeboat station to sit on the cliff-edge of the golf course (no golfers) and watch the seals coming to roost out there on the rocks. And they do, again.

Michael Haslam used to sing to these seals. We don't, but in our silent hearts we shout over to them, "Hey, seals, remember us? You haven't seen us for four years now but we always came here. And you were here in those days, seals, we watched you out there on the rocky pinnacles, your home for the night. Every year we came here since the baby was born, eighteen years and now the twenty-second. How are you getting on, seals? It looks good, there's more of you than ever. Big ones and little ones, rolling about on the sharp rock needles with nothing but seaweed to comfort your hides. Snorting and puffing and calming down as the light goes. And being there, at rest on a known point, being there tonight again. We think it's a great achievement, seals. Can you hear me? We think it's the answer."

> Remember you too were once a new-born baby
> as helpless as a seal on a rock just
> rolling around while war flew
> red banners over the green city.

7) Reading books or playing scrabble while the water hurls itself at the thin walls and the whole edifice shakes slightly. The two sheep in the field outside looking perfectly happy about it, standing still in the rain. Two hand-reared lambs who run up to you if you enter their field, two friends, two siblings... Reminding me, that there are two honest attitudes to what's happening in the world, birth-joined in a hatred of injustice, but rigorously opposed to each other. The buyers and the sellers. Those who scan and those who focus. And that something else, like a sheep-ness, arches over them both and keeps them persevering in the same field. A balance, a conflict, created in this recognition which generates the tension on which the song is sung.

> Only the song stands high to see
> on stones of the yard on the message wire
> stands and calls, brushes water from coat,
> everything said returns to the throat
>
> Making there its nest, red cell cluster that
> closes the light and leaves the land
> quiet under vast rain vast under spread pain
> lapping the edges of a modern caravan again.

Later it won't matter what these words mean
in the light of what these words seem a cat
on a wall a rook on a wire a sheep in a field a
hope lost in the pink world home to its believer.

And the long land with white houses proposes
a symmetry to your warring poses and the answer lies
all round you. A little flock of some little bird or other
over the rain beaten bushes flares and falls together.

Do so and melt. *Zerschmilts, du felsenhartes Hertze!*
Everything said runs back to the throat, and
works there a form of gain. A security brighter
than the fields, and harder than the rain.

A solitude which is gained, a safety in a shortness
of time, curved to the sky and turning round and
round again a chaconne which we bird voices
trill over in flight, settling to the bar of night.

A solitary night together, all of us. Towards
the end of which a passing luminous creature
spreads a call over the roof concerning death that cause
of fear. Wrapped in distance we count it ever more dear.

13

LLŶN, PAUSING AND GOING

Llŷn, Pausing

That peculiarly broken ground, the turf cover always halting at an earthen scoop. Shoulders of grass above the sea clasped tight in mosses, plantains, clumps of thrift, opening like wounds to reveal the grey rock surface. The bright orange lichen on the stone roofs, the rust breaking through the green-painted corrugated iron. The tall stony banks between fields, hawthorn hedges along the roads, with elder and blackthorn, riding into stream hollows and up again. Sections planned and executed long ago, long fields riding the waves of land to break at the littoral. Solid thick-walled stone houses with small windows and front porches, and here and there makeshift dwellings made of boards with tin roofs tucked into field corners with a gate through the hedge from the road. And the lives there, entire lives which cannot be reduced to their occasions, but seeming to have almost nothing of their own, no ornament. And there is no dictionary to explain the terms, of this great distance, of these bare walls, of these flat hats tilted over physical tasks.

Only the chapels, bare outside and in, with the low graves set round them, partaking of the same austerity as the fields and houses. The care for the polished wood, the rule of no ornament. A hymn in Welsh reaching us through the thick walls, pushed around by the wind over the fields as we bend over Goronwy's grave, sung plainly and in perfect steadiness. I don't see, in my fifty-ninth year, that we have anything better to offer, in the ever burgeoning contrarieties of our cosmopolitan riches, than a place set apart where someone with the job in hand will tell you it is all right, it has to be, sing together and rejoice. Or a doctor who will tell you, I'm sorry, but it is not all right.

And the choughs, not knowing they are choughs and so quite special, seen from time to time, always in pairs, floating over the cliff ends, and we notice with pleasure that they have children. They have children in foul weather, and attend to them in niches of the cliff as sheets of rain sweep along the coast. And next year they are there again, flying over the sea where seals, uninterested in choughs, cast their eyes downwards through the water. And following their sight, turn into the deep. Seeking food, as we, seeking rest, or adventure, turn into our graves.

Llŷn, Going

Going away now. The chances diminish,
of returning. I wonder if my daughter
will bring her children here, and find
a Mrs Jones still here. Me not here, me
somewhere else

Singing my hymn. Lift up your heart
and your voice. I wonder if the sound
will reach the far shore, I wonder
if the sea's continual code will ever
be broken, in English or Welsh,

Someone, dead or alive, saying, in
either language or any on earth,
that like the stars in the morning
sky we reckon to falter and cease,
and place what we know on a broken shelf

"Only remembered for what we have done."
High voices in the cove, excited at the
splashing waves, running towards them
and back, three kittens on the farm wall,
singing in the wire, love grows in the sun.

And the day grows beyond love or hope
into its result sure and firm in the
lowering farmlight. A future running
towards me across a field, that I myself
helped to grow and be, shadows on the sea.

Addenda & Notes to

Sea Watches

1. *Sea Watches*: The Blurb

The following text by the author was issued by Prest Roots Press as a flyer for Sea Watches *in 1991.*

A person finds him/herself, year after year, in an ancient landscape. It is a peninsula in North Wales pointing to an unreachable island. Pilgrims' goal, rock of ages, ecstatic finality. What do you do about that? What do you bring to bear on this sense of ageing purpose begging to be renewed? How do you attempt to validate presence against cracked dreams? Proud bodies zip past you on motorised skis. World politics lurks far round the coast selling plastic corn flakes to the survivors. What do you say? Ordinary things. Common musings. Focused thoughts such as anyone might have, any member of a family coming and going, eating and trading, noticing the shore curving into fate, troubled by the multi-distance of the sea, its hoarse voice referring persistently to absent time.

I set this scenario in a poetical structure to find out what more happened to what it was possible to say when it breathed more deeply and longly, in numerical order. A pact with the sea's motor.

2. *Sea Watches*: Rhyme

In the first edition was a "Note on the verse form" which is not reprinted here. It pointed out among other things that (with rare exception) the stanzas of *Sea Watches* rhyme alternately ABCDEF, "which means that the end-rhymes are twelve lines apart and cannot without difficulty be held in the reader's memory. Their function is thus structural rather than melodic..." The concept "rhyme" which is explored in this text also includes half-rhymes, false rhymes, internal rhymes, and "semantic rhymes", which is my own term for two words which "chime together" because they are closely related in their definitions and for no other reason. There is also a habit of displacing the second of a pair of end-rhymes to a penultimate syllable, as a way of leading the text on rhymically.

3. Topographical Notes to *Sea Watches*

(Written to accompany the first edition of Sea Watches, *these notes also supply a geographical and historical context for all the other writings in this collection, as well as constituting a mental ramble over the terrain.)*

These stanzas are all set in North Wales, on the Llŷn Peninsula, with some excursions northwards up the coast. A caravan at a small coastal farm called Rhwngyddwyborth ("between two coves") on the north side of the peninsula a few miles from its end was visited one week in each of thirteen years 1977-1989, during which this poem accumulated, initially as an exercise in remote rhyme. Visits have variously been in May, August, and October, which accounts for seasonal inconsistencies in different parts of the text. Most of the stanzas were drafted in a pocket note-book, or a pocket brain, at the places mentioned in the text or notes.

All references to pilgrimage throughout are to Bardsey Island which lies two miles off the end of the peninsula. (The Welsh name, Ynys Enlli, is little used.) The peninsula, which trends south-west under Anglesey as an extension of the geology of the Snowdon Range, does not taper to a point, but narrows along its twelve-mile length and then broadens, ending in a boss of hills with precipitous cliffs to the sea on all sides, beyond which Bardsey rides the sea as a further hill, a ruined abbey on its gentler side.

Bardsey is said to have been at one time secondary only to Canterbury or St David's as a place of pilgrimage within Britain (three Bardseys equalled one Rome) but is now virtually uninhabited and difficult of access. The pilgrimages were initiated by Augustinians in the 13th Century, by which time the island already had a reputation as a special, sacred or remanent site, free from diseases, home of extreme old age. It was originally a reclusory flung out from a monastic settlement on the mainland near Aberdaron and later occasionally a refuge for dispossessed monastic communities. Once established as a goal of pilgrimage it became extremely popular, and the approaches to it by sea and land, now so quiet but for the unoriented buzz of tourism in the season, must have been laden with traffic and catering for hundreds of years. The two land routes along the peninsula, cutting across all the local trans-peninsular trade routes, can still be traced with ease, marked by series of chapels, but much of the traffic was by sea. The tradition that twenty thousand saints are buried on the island might seem to imply that sainthood was conferred by little more than arrival, but there was also a haulage industry transporting coffined corpses to Bardsey from all over Britain. The island seems not to have had any prestigious relics or holy ghosts to account for its success, and the very difficulty of reaching it seems to have been the main part of the attraction –

"It is called the Welsh Rome because of the long and dangerous journey to the very end of the kingdom, and because of the holiness and purity of the place."
(The Life of Edgar the Hermit)

The straits between the mainland and Bardsey are among the most difficult passages on the coast of Britain, subject to conflicting currents and winds which can whip up high seas very quickly and with little warning. See Brenda Chamberlain's account of her survival of a crossing, in *Tide-Race*.

The sequences of stanzas edge slowly towards the sight of Bardsey, but with many tactics of diversion and recoil. The caravan is a mere hour's walk from Uwchmynydd ("high hill"), the principal mountain marking the end of the peninsula, but all excursions before set VII are either minimal or directed back and/or across.

The first set approaches Llŷn on the northern route from Caernarfon, pausing on the top of the mountain pass at Llithfaen where on a clear day the entire peninsula can be seen laid out in front of you (I/1), then moving down into the vicinity of the caravan, stopping at Porth Or (I/3) and the rest of I is set in the caravan itself or on the small coastal cliffs in its vicinity. The marble boulder in I/4 was at Porth Witlin and later, rather oddly, wasn't. Re I/7 is may be helpful to note that some caravans have a central table which converts into a bed by lowering the board and joining it to the side benches.

Set II represents a sedentary day not far from the farm,

mostly at Porth Or (English name Whistling Sands), an isolated beach-bay popular enough to support the small shop mentioned in I/3. II/1 is on a short cut to this bay, a disused track confused with a dry stream, during an October visit. II/2-3 are on the beach during the high season. II/4-5 is a solo walk over the cliff-top pastures to the next cove north, Porth Iago, but II/6 returns to Whistling Sands. The very fine light cream sand does indeed squeak under the foot on dry days. The quotation in II/7 is adapted from Brenda Chamberlain, in *Tide-Race*, talking of her reclusion on Bardsey, which is where the moon sets in II/8.

Re II/3, the noise level on a busy beach with active waves is high, and if the sound spectrum is studied strange aural hallucinations can be observed, such as high-pitched singing voices seeming to come from the direction of the sea, intermittently appearing and disappearing over the roar of waves. I think this effect must be the product of the welter of mostly high-pitched human voices (excited children etc.) and the sound of the sea breaking. Probably the voices from the beach merge into the upper harmonics of the noise of waves and echo themselves over the sea transformed into a choir of mermaids. The chorus mentioned in II/5 is not this effect, but the much fuller mingled drone of two crowds in the distance as heard from the cliff-top pastures between the two bays.

In English these places are usually called beach, bay, or cove, but the sea has always been a workplace in this country, and the Welsh "porth / borth" actually translates as "harbour".

III/2-5 move across to the other, south, coast of Llŷn. Hell's Mouth is the old English name of Porth Neigwl, an almost straight three-mile bay on Cardigan Bay with a bad reputation for shipwrecks; as a flat area between high promontories it constantly attracts wind and is almost never calm. The area surrounding it shows plentiful evidence of the first human (Neolithic) settlement on the peninsula. III/4 is in the steep sheltered valley leading down to Porth Ysgo, a cove in the west promontory of Hell's Mouth. The mines referred to are manganese workings abandoned in the 19th Century.

III/6-7 are about angling for mackerel from the farm in a small outboard-motor boat called "Pilgrim", and are mementoes of the fisherman/farmer host, who died suddenly in January 1990. A gentleman, of meticulous calm, and inimitable skills.

Set IV escapes entirely from the peninsula in a solo excursion northwards, back along the approach route and on up the coast, which I undertook most years in connection with my occupation as a second-hand bookseller: through Nefyn, Llithfaen, Clynnog, (by some lapse or warp IV/1 and IV/3 are both in the vicinity of Clynnog whereas IV/2 is already further up the coast) to Caernarfon, Bangor, Llandudno and Bethesda. This area beyond the border of Llŷn presents a long history of exploitation and occupation from which Llŷn itself was more or less exempt – English castles, estates, watering-places, amusement parks, new world encampments, quarries all over the place mostly now abandoned. Bethesda (IV/4-5) sits in an enormous arena of defunct slate quarries. The return is by a hilly back route from here (IV/6) to rejoin the family at the only pub within miles of the caravan (IV/7).

Set V represents a much shorter excursion, just over the border of Llŷn to the north. V/2-3 concern Porth y Nant, a large-scale bay at the foot of the mountain mass (Yr Eifl) containing Llithfaen, full of the remains of a large gravel and slate industry. It is cut off from the land: the mountain rises directly from the shore some 1000 feet and there was never any road access to the bay or the now abandoned village on a shelf at its north end. The gravel and stones were poured down the hillside in chutes to loading piers and removed by ship. V/2 in approaching this arena deliberately avoids the road recently blasted down to the old village and takes a little used trackway over the coastal heights to the south, on which stands the sleeping-beauty house. (See *Llŷn in the Rain* 5 for the more recent condition of this area, which is also referred to as Nant Gwrtheyrn (the village) and Porth Gwrtheyrn (the bay).)

V/4 rejoins company at Nefyn, shifting in V/5-6 to its resort companion Morfa Nefyn in an environment of sea-sports and long established beach-houses, some of them on stilts over the sand. The author admits to being rather fascinated by this kind of milieu, as a regular holiday location proper to the mid-century English middle-class family, which he aspired to through reading Enid Blyton. The terraced garden in V/6 is not here but is suddenly remembered from Plas yn Rhiw near the end of the peninsula. It was created by a couple of English women who settled there in the 1940s.

Other than Bryn Celli Ddu the sites of VII are all pilgrimage chapels of rest or stations along the northern or southern peninsular routes to Aberdaron and Bardsey. The chapels are usually sited a little inland near the heads of small coastal valleys to be near streams. Although some serve as parish churches they are mostly well separated from the villages, and some fell into disuse when pilgrimages ended and have not survived. As well as foot pilgrims they served sea transport to and from nearby coves and some of them, perhaps those which seem ill sites for catering facilities, must have been more specifically designed to serve the corpse haulage industry. That at Pistyll (VII/1) best preserves the original aspect of its site, with a stream running by it and the oval churchyard still bearing ash, wild fruit bushes and hops for food and drink, and "daneberry" (dwarf elder) which was said to ease the transmigration of souls.

Pistyll is at the south foot of the mountain from Llithfaen, on the border of Llŷn. These days the guardians of the little church keep it full of picked plants at all times, chiefly medicinal herbs. Llangwnnadl is the nearest parish to the north of Rhwngddwyborth, the church a fine light and spacious triple-aisled perpendicular structure. The site of St Merin's church is a hundred yards south of the caravan in the middle of a field. Llandudwen is somewhat back to the centre of the peninsula and was indeed built over the grave of an aunt of St David, though the primary focus of the site was a spring. Capel Anelog has vanished without trace but I think it was at the north-east foot of Mynydd Anelog, a dignified conical hill impinging on Uwchmynydd, and would have been an important penultimate station on a foot route which all pilgrims may have had to take however they arrived at the end of the peninsula. Before that it was the centre of the original monastic settlement of which Bardsey was an outlier: the meeting hall or pre-temple in a scatter of cells, on the Judean model. Ffynnon Fair (St Mary's Well) is traditionally an embarkment point for Bardsey at the foot of the cliffs of

Uwchmynydd. It is reached by a precipitous track and steps carved in the rock of the cliff face, and consists only of an untidy collection of rock strata on which the sea is always breaking with force. There is a freshwater spring in a natural stoup on the cliff face, and it is said that if the place is approached from the sea it can be identified by a likeness of the Virgin on the cliff face above it. It is difficult to imagine hundreds of people, and coffins, embarking and disembarking daily at this cramped and dangerous spot, but it retains the repute of a principal harbour for pilgrims to Bardsey and a chapel is named on the cliff tops above it, which if it survives at all is now a few linear humps among bracken.

Bryn Celli Ddu (Dark Grove Mound) is the furthest distant of any of the sites involved in this poem. It is on Anglesey, near the middle of the south coast, and is one of the class of Neolithic structures generally known as "chambered tombs", a definition now open to question.

Set VIII returns to the vicinity of the caravan and represents a night-long sea watch in a grassy niche exactly the size and shape of an armchair, which I discovered in 1989 half way up the cliff in the somewhat desolate (pre-Cambrian) area to the north of the farm. This was undertaken five successive nights, here conflated into one, during which the moon moved from late three-quarters to full and was eclipsed. The equipment of these vigils was: pencil, notebook, binoculars, waterproof cape with hood, camera, half a pound of blue Stilton cheese, and a personal stereo system with six tapes. The music was by Sheppard, de Sermisy, Hildegard of Bingen, Purcell, Derek Bailey, and the Chinese zither known as chîn or gukin.

4.
Welsh pronunciation cannot be gone into here. But two points may be noted –
1) There is a thing called the mutation of initial consonants, whereby "porth" and "borth" for instance, are the same word, as are "tad" and "dad" (father), mutated according to grammatical function. Nine consonants mutate and three of them can have four different forms.
2) About the time we first started going to Llŷn a correct

Welsh orthography started appearing on road signs and other places, so that what had been Caernarvon became Caernarfon. Overheard conversation in tea-shops confirmed that the English immediately started pronouncing it "Carnarffon". But the Welsh single F is voiced and the anglicised form reflected this by using V.

5. Other Notes

Six Prose Pieces. On the two churches mentioned here see *Sea Watches* VII, notes.

page 28. There is a legend about St Merin's church which I half-remembered from a conversation with a Mr Roberts of Aberdaron, in his living-room, which doubled as the waiting-room of the doctor's surgery twice a week. It was about a thief stealing St Merin's silver bell and leaping over the coastal rocks carrying it until divine intervention dropped him into a sea crevice.

Poems and Notes. page 35. cloth of gold. An old poetic epithet for Llŷn, referring to the profusion of gorse bushes or, more likely, the fertility of the land.

page 36. the Vicar of Aberdaron: R.S. Thomas, who lived in retirement at Rhiw above Hell's Mouth. This poem is in part a collage of phrases and notions from his poems, with that particularly stony, exposed and sea-light-stricken place in mind.

pages 39-41 Porth Gwrtheyrn, Porth y Nant. See *Sea Watches* V, note.

Sea Watches Overstock. page 45 hilltop citadels. The mainland of Llŷn is lowland in character but for igneous outcrops forming a series of dignified conical hills down the spine of the peninsula, with a prehistoric settlement on the top of each, now visible mainly as plentiful clusters of stone hut-circles. Tre'r Ceiri, Garn Boduan, Carn Fadrun, Castell Odo, etc. There is recorded and legendary later use of these hilltop sites, some of it rather bizarre.

page 46. Phil Davenport: see *Alstonefield: a poem* (2003) p.42

Night-watch Notebook. see *Sea Watches* VIII note. It will be noticed that the music mentioned here does not correspond exactly to the list given there. This might be explained by the fact that the personal stereo system included a radio receiver.

page 49. "Death should not be a problem…" slightly adapted from Norbert Elias, The Loneliness of Dying (1985)

Sea Watch Elegies. The first edition bore a note after the text quoting the note to *Sea Watches* III/6-7, "the fisherman/farmer host…"

Overheard by the Sea. This is the remains of a work originally conceived as a poetical dialogue between my son and my father on the cliff tops overlooking the shore at Porth y Nant; that is, eliminating myself into a vacuum between them. Its fictive basis was an apocalyptic scenario, as of a destroyed country from which they were waiting to be rescued by boat.

Llŷn in the Rain
page 104. *Zerschmilts, du felsenhartes Hertze!* "Melt, you stone-hard heart!" Opening of a song from the opera *Cecrops* by Johann Philipp Krieger (1649-1725). See also *A Map of Faring* (2005) p.14 and note.

Llŷn, Going. "Only remembered…" and "shadows on the sea" are both phrases from songs, and both have been used in several other poems. The former is traditional, the latter the title of a song by Joe Skilbeck sung by The Men of Staithes, which used to be a fishermen's choir before the fishing stopped on the east coast of England. It refers to an old belief that that is what sailors' (and presumably fishermen's) souls became if they did not become seagulls. The ending of *Overheard by the Sea* is also influenced by one of his songs, "Heading for the Harbour Lights".

Bibliography

Geraldus di Barri called Cambrensis, Itinerarium Cambriae. various translations.

Brenda Chamberlaine, *Tide Race*. 1961

Kenneth Hurlstone Jackson, *A Celtic Miscellany*. 1971 (re St. Columba)

C.N. Johns, "The Celtic Monasteries of North Wales". *Transactions of the Caernarvonshire Historical Society* 19, 1958

T. Pierce Jones, "Bardsey — a study in monastic origins." *Transactions of the Caernarvonshire Historical Society* 24, 1963

Molly Miller, *The Saints of Gwynedd*. 1979

Roy Millward and Adrian Robinson, *Landscapes of North Wales*. 1978

Andrew O'Hagan, *The End of British Farming*. 2001

Over the Stile: 32 walks in the Llyn. Bramble Press, Pwllheli 1980

St Beuno's Church Pystyll. Anonymous mimeographed leaflet obtained in the church.

www.ingramcontent.com/pod-product-compliance
Lightning Source LLC
Chambersburg PA
CBHW031155160426
43193CB00008B/374